Practical
Business
Letters

By the same authors:
Commercial Correspondence in English (Nelson)

M D Spooner
J S McKellen

Practical
Business
Letters

Nelson

Thomas Nelson and Sons Ltd
Nelson House Mayfield Road
Walton-on-Thames Surrey KT12 5PL

51 York Place
Edinburgh EH1 3JD

P.O. Box 18123
Nairobi Kenya

Yi Xiu Factory Building
Unit 05-06 5th Floor
65 Sims Avenue Singapore 1438

Thomas Nelson (Hong Kong) Ltd
Toppan Bldg 10/F 22A Westlands Road
Quarry Bay Hong Kong

Thomas Nelson (Nigeria) Ltd
8 Ilupeju Bypass PMB 21303 Ikeja Lagos

© M D Spooner and J S McKellen 1978
First published by Thomas Nelson and Sons Ltd 1978
Reprinted 1980, 1981, 1982, 1983
ISBN 0-17-555051-4
NCN 760-8505-4

Printed in Hong Kong

Contents

Introduction

This book has been written to help the elementary student to write acceptable and comprehensible business letters in English, and to understand letters he receives, which will be written in ordinary, colloquial English. We are assuming that the reader will be living abroad and that he needs to write to English people in his line of business; the book can also be used for students on short courses in this country. The structures he is to use are kept within an upper elementary level (as far as possible they are those which are included within the first book of a three-book course or the first book and a half of a four-book course) and the vocabulary is kept as simple as possible except for business terms, which the student will have to understand if not to use; difficult words or words used with a special commercial meaning are marked with an asterisk in the text the first time they appear, and explained in the Glossary at the end of the book. Since the student will have to understand letters written in ordinary English, more difficult than he can use himself, we have introduced the most common terms and structures deliberately, even though he is at a fairly elementary level.

The choice of items for inclusion in this book is based on what the student needs for communication with English firms. It owes much to the notional approach, now becoming well established in English Language Teaching. It is intended to be a book which will enable the student to adapt his knowledge of the English language to his need to write and understand the English used in business. Structural concepts, with a rare exception such as the use of 'would like' rather than 'want', are not explained; the whole object of the book is to allow the student to become fluent in using simple, correct English.

There are far more examples than explanations (except in the chapter on payment, where a good deal of explanation is necessary), and the exercises are designed to make the student use and understand the information in the book and adapt it to his own needs. It is hoped that students will, after working through the book, be able to make enquiries from an English firm, order what they require and pay for it, and that they will be able to understand the letters they receive. They will obviously need to be able to comprehend more than they need to use, and as much explanation as necessary has been given to help in this.

To help the student plan his letters we have used the 'three-paragraph' approach throughout – an introductory paragraph explaining what the letter is about and replying to any previous correspondence, a middle paragraph containing the body of the letter, and a final paragraph summing up and explaining what needs to be done next – as a basis for constructing letters. We feel that this will help the student to think what he is going to say and plan the way in which he is going to say it. He should, therefore, be able to say it simply, correctly and clearly.

The authors would like to thank their colleagues for help and advice throughout the preparation of this book.

M D Spooner
Cambridge 1977

J S McKellen
London 1977

1. Writing English Letters

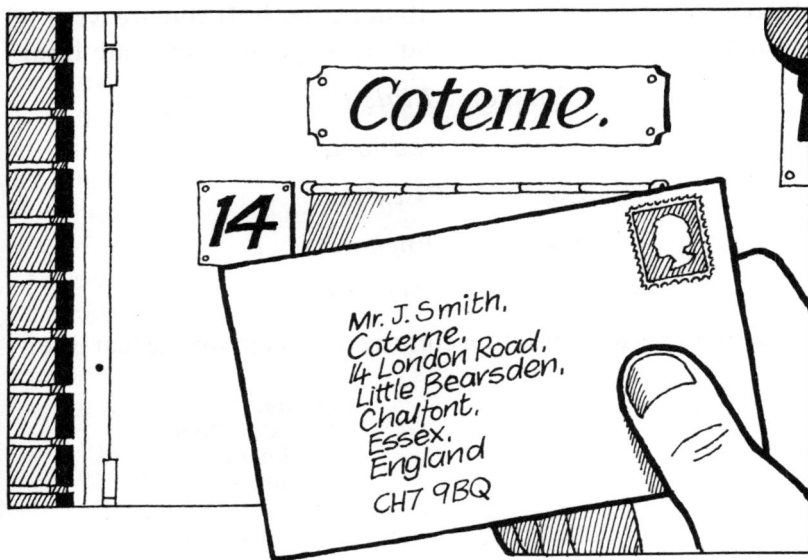

In this book you will find simple ways to write letters which are easy to remember. They are always correct.

First you must write your address. In England you do not write your name before your address at the head of a letter (although you do on an envelope), and you write the address on the right-hand side of the page (some firms have theirs printed in the centre) at the beginning of the letter.

The name of the house, if it has one, (on a separate line) and the number of the house are written first, followed by the name of the road or street, like this:

name of house		*Coterne,*
number and road (Rd.)		*14 London Rd.,*
or street (St.)	or	*14 Brighton St.,*
or avenue (Ave.)	or	*14 Exeter Ave.,*

You then write the name of the town and the county. If the town is very large and well-known, like London or Manchester, it is not necessary to write the name of the county. (A list of common abbreviations for the counties will be found at the end of this chapter on p. 7.) The town (or county) is followed by the postcode, which has no full-stop after it. If you are writing from another country 'England' must be on a separate line:

(Village)	*(Little Bearsden,)*
Town	*Chalfont,*
County	*Essex(,)*
(Country)	*(England)*
Postcode	*CH7 9BQ*

Each line is followed by a comma (,), except for the last line:

Coterne,
14 London Road,
Little Bearsden,
Chalfont,
Essex,
England CH7 9BQ

However some firms are using open punctuation (that is, without any commas in the address).

On the envelope the postcode must always be the last line with a space after the line above. (This is because more and more sorting offices are being mechanised and it is the bottom line that is recorded mechanically.)

The date is normally written under the address; the day is followed by the month and then the year. The date is usually written with ordinal numbers.* However, dates written 14 August 1977 or 1 January 1978 are acceptable, as are the shortened forms: 14.8.1977 (or 14.8.77) and 1.1.1978 (or 1.1.78).

Note: In America, the month is written before the day. So the shortened form from America of June 2 1975 is 6.2.75; in the English use, 6.2.75 would be 6 February 1975.

Below your address, but on the left-hand side of the page, you should write the name and address of the person you are writing to. (If you do not know his or her name, use the name of his/her job: The Manager, The Secretary, etc.) So the address would look like this:

```
The Manager,
Weald Park Hotel,
Hendon,
London N4 5EU
```

or

```
Mr John Smith,
Hyde Travel Bureau,
51 High Street,
Manchester MA51 3ZX
```

or

```
The Secretary,
Martin and Rhodes Ltd.,
25 King Street,
Beston,
Montshire,
England TH2 9UO
```

The most usual way to start the letter is by writing 'Dear . . .,'. This is written against the left-hand margin (not in the centre) of the first line, and is followed by a comma, not a full stop or exclamation mark (!). There is a space between the last line of the address and this. (In America most letters start with 'My Dear . . .,'.)

```
Mr John Smith,
Hyde Travel Bureau,
51 High Street,
Manchester MA51 3ZX

Dear . . .,
```

If you are writing to one person (The Manager, The Secretary,) you say 'Dear Sir,'. If you are writing to more than one person in a firm, you say 'Dear Sirs,'. If you start by writing 'Dear Sir,' or 'Dear Sirs,' you must finish with 'Yours faithfully,' as shown in the examples on pp. 5–6. If you know the name of the person to whom you are writing, you begin 'Dear Mr Smith,' and finish 'Yours sincerely,'. If you are writing to a lady you say 'Dear Mrs Brown,' or 'Dear Miss Green,'; if you do not know whether she is married or not, you can use 'Ms'. If you do not know her name, begin your letter with 'Dear Madam,' (*not* 'Dear Miss,' or 'Dear Mrs,').

Note: In England the family name follows the forename. An English person will usually write to someone using the last name of the signature, so it is best to follow the English style, even if it seems strange to you, if you do not wish to be addressed as 'Dear Mr Giovanni'.

Most business letters have three paragraphs. The first is usually short, explaining what the letter is about. It may also thank your correspondent for his letter:

> I have seen your advertisement for 'Airman' shoes. I am writing to ask about the colours you make them in.

> or

> Thank you for your letter of 14th August 19—, sending me your catalogue.

A second paragraph explains what you need, and asks any other questions:

> I do not want black or brown shoes, but if you make blue or green shoes, I shall write and order three pairs for myself and my friends.

A third paragraph explains what you would like the firm to do:

> When I have your answer, I will write and send an International Money Order for the shoes. I will also tell you which sizes we need.

A space is left above the ending of the letter, 'Yours faithfully,' or 'Yours sincerely,' which is written on the next line, either against the left-hand margin or in the centre, according to your normal layout.

In general, every new idea should have its own paragraph (this is difficult for non-English people to understand, but the rule is really very simple). So, although most business letters are about one main subject and therefore have one main paragraph as well as an introductory paragraph and a closing paragraph, some letters may need two or three paragraphs in the body* of the letter. This is unusual, however.

Your letter, therefore, will look like this when it is finished:

Viale S. Antonio n. 129,
Milano 78347,
Italia.

10.10.19—

The Sales Manager,
Boswell Foods Limited,
Grange Road,
Moretown,
England ME14 7AB

Dear Sir,

When I visited your country last week I sampled some of
your special 'Savoury Cheese', and I should like to know if
you can let me have regular supplies.

I own a number of hotels and if your cheese is popular I
hope to place large orders with you.

I hope to hear from you soon.

Yours faithfully,

P. Steffanelli

P. Steffanelli

The layout for this letter is blocked – each new paragraph
starts against the left-hand margin. It is equally correct to use
an indented layout – when each new paragraph starts a few
spaces from the left-hand margin. (See the letter on p. 6.) Some
typists can choose which layout they prefer, but some firms
insist that all their letters are set out in the same way.

6

Another letter looks like this:

Casa Bazaar,
8 Rue Nolly,
Tangier, Morocco.

12th September 19—

The Manager,
Lynton Leather Co., Ltd.,
71 Thorpe Street,
Lynton,
Southshire,
England NE21 5GJ

Dear Sir,
   Thank you for your letter of 5th September enclosing your catalogue.
   We are very interested in your 'Rosedale' range* of briefcases. We would be glad if you could send us twenty (20) of the large size. If these sell well we shall send a further order.
   We hope to receive these goods within 21 days as stated in your letter.

Yours faithfully,

A. El Karem

Or the letter could be slightly shortened to :

Dear Sir,
   Thank you for your catalogue.
   We should like to order twenty (20) large size 'Rosedale' briefcases. A further order will follow if these goods are satisfactory.
   We look forward to receiving the briefcases within 21 days as stated in your letter.

Yours faithfully,

From now on, we will not repeat the details of your address. You have learned how to write addresses in England, but most of your business letters to English firms will be written from your own country, so that you will simply write your own address as you normally do, unless you use your firm's printed notepaper.*

Sometimes it is possible to shorten the spelling of the county, and the following abbreviations should be used:

Beds	Bedfordshire	N. Humberside	North Humberside
Berks	Berkshire	Northd	Northumberland
Bucks	Buckinghamshire	N. Yorkshire	North Yorkshire
Cambs	Cambridgeshire	Notts	Nottinghamshire
Derry	Londonderry	Oxon	Oxfordshire
Co. Durham	County Durham	S. Glam	South Glamorgan
E. Sussex	East Sussex	S. Humberside	South Humberside
Glos	Gloucestershire	S. Yorkshire	South Yorkshire
Hants	Hampshire	Staffs	Staffordshire
Herts	Hertfordshire	Tyne & Wear	Tyne and Wear
Lancs	Lancashire	W. Glam	West Glamorgan
Leics	Leicestershire	W. Midlands	West Midlands
Lincs	Lincolnshire	W. Sussex	West Sussex
Middx	Middlesex	W. Yorkshire	West Yorkshire
M. Glam	Mid Glamorgan	Wilts	Wiltshire
Northants	Northamptonshire	Worcs	Worcestershire

Exercises

1 Write the following addresses in the English style:
(a) Cambridgeshire/High Street/Great Eversden/CB3 7HN/ 4
(b) HA1 3JJ / Road / London / 9 / Middlesex / Harrow
(c) Bath Avenue / Broadlands / Highgate / 3 /
   London / N41 4EU
(d) Road / Ainsdale / PO14 2QX / Portsmouth / Drayton /
   7 / Hampshire
(e) Lincoln Way / Sunbury-on-Thames / SH60 0AH /
   Middlesex / Windmill Road

2 Begin a letter to:
(a) The Sales Manager of Moses Tinker, Petty Street, Cambridge CB6 8JM

(b) Mr John Rhodes, Managing Director, Williams and Co., Ltd., Knapwell House, Ely St., Oxford OX22 1BJ
(c) The Manageress, Rondo Cafe, 46 High Street, Bath, Somerset BA19 2ST
(d) The Works Manager, Lowsons Agricultural Products Ltd., 319 Upper Road, Manchester MA52 3OZ
(e) The Secretary, Hilton Products Ltd., 521 Straight St., Stevenage, Herts ST15 6XJ

3 End a letter to:
(a) The Sales Manager
(b) Mr T. Brown, Managing Director
(c) Ms J. Jones, Secretary
(d) Mrs C. Williams, Manageress
(e) The Editor, Cambridge Morning Mail

4 Begin a letter to each of the people named in Exercise 3.

5 You are Mr F. Brown, The Manager, The Queens Head Hotel, Lower Harrow, Middlesex HA12 2ST. You are writing to The Marketing Manager, Thomsons Linen Co., Ltd., 6 North Square, Southport, Cheshire ST40 1NT. Write out both addresses and the beginning and ending of the letter.

2. Letters of Enquiry and Replying to Them. Becoming an Agent

Enquiries

Letters of enquiry are written when you would like to find out about a product*, such as china, furniture or shoes. You will usually want to know the price and how long the product will take to reach you; you may also want to know something else about its quality*. You will also often want to ask how you can open an account* with a firm, and what are the terms of business*.

You begin as explained in the previous chapter:

The Manager,
Barcus Shoe Company Limited,
159 High Street,
Aldenham,
Southshire AL5 3NM

As you do not know the manager's name, you start:

Dear Sir,

In your first paragraph, you explain why you are writing:

I went to the exhibition of English shoes last week, and saw the shoes made by your firm. I would like* to know more about them.

In your second paragraph, you explain in detail what you would like to know:

> I have a store in the centre of Paris, and deal in* smart models at popular prices. I think your 'Seltona' range is exactly what I need, and I am writing to ask the price of these shoes in various sizes. I would also like to know how long they will take to reach me after you receive my order, and if you have any other shoes like them. I expect to order 100 pairs of each.

The third paragraph of the letter tells the person to whom you are writing what you would like him to do:

> I look forward to hearing from you.

Since the letter starts 'Dear Sir,' it ends, of course:

> Yours faithfully,

Here is another example of a letter of enquiry:

16th June 19—

The Manager,
Glenloch Tweed Mills Ltd.,
29/31 Campbell Street,
Acol,
Scotland ED29 5GP

Dear Sir,

I recently saw some samples of your 'White Heather' tweed cloth which could be made into ladies' skirts. I would be grateful if you would send me full details of this material.

We have a large tailoring department and would like to stock* a new type of material. I would like to know the price for a metre and also how soon the material will arrive. If your terms* are favourable I shall probably order about 1,000 metres, and more in future.

I hope to hear from you soon.

Yours faithfully,

Jean Gerard

Jean Gerard
Tailoring Department Manager

Note: In many firms or businesses where one man or woman has a special job, such as Secretary, Sales Manager, Accountant, etc., it is usual to state his or her position at the end of the letter after the signature. Sometimes it is difficult to read the signature, and if it is typed as well as written, there can be no misunderstanding. (In the rest of this book we shall refer to *he* or *him*, but the reader should understand that this is short for *he/she* or *him/her*.)

Now here is a reply to the letter received from Mr Jean Gerard:

22nd June 19——

Monsieur Jean Gerard,
Maison Renault,
67 Av. de la Reine,
09510 Paris,
France.

Dear Mr Gerard,
    Thank you for your letter of 16th June 19—— enquiring about our 'White Heather' tweed.
    I enclose a catalogue and samples of the full range of colours and the cost per* metre. We usually carry large stocks* and could despatch the material within two weeks from the date of receiving your order. We should be very pleased to do business* with you and would ask you to let us have the usual trade and bank references.*
    I hope the catalogue gives all the information you need, but please do not hesitate to write again if you would like any further details.

Yours sincerely,

Duncan Campbell

Duncan Campbell
Manager

Here is a possible reply to the letter on p. 5:

Signore P. Steffanelli,
Viale S. Antonio n. 129,
Milan 78347,
Italy.   16th October 19—

Dear Mr Steffanelli,
    Thank you for your letter of 10th October 19—.
    We are delighted that you like our 'Savoury Cheese' and
would like to order some for your hotel. We will send the
cheese as soon as we receive your order. The cheese is
packed in 25 kilogramme boxes at a cost of £75.60 per box.
If you open an account with us there will be a discount of
5% for all orders over £200, and a further 5% if accounts*
are settled within 30 days.
    I hope these terms are agreeable to you and I look
forward to receiving an order from you.

                        Yours sincerely,

                        Peter Jones
                        Sales Manager

Here are some more examples; the first is very general and
could be used for almost any commodity.*

The Manager,
The Country Produce Centre,
Lowsford,
Mountshire,
England GL5 9DJ   24th January 19—

Dear Sir,

When I was visiting England a few weeks ago I saw some
of your excellent products. I should like to order some to
sell in my country. Please send me a catalogue and price
list, and tell me your terms of business and delivery date.

I look forward to hearing from you.

Yours faithfully,

P. Schoenenberger
P. Schoenenberger
Marketing* Manager

Here is a reply to this letter:

The Country Produce Centre Ltd.

Lowsford,
Mountshire,
England GL5 9DJ

Tel: Lowsford 95381
VAT Reg. No. 25 375 4957

Herrn P. Schoenenberger,
Gartenstrasse 153,
D–978 Gottschalk,
Germany.   31st January 19—— ·

Dear Mr Schoenenberger,
    Thank you for your letter of 24th January 19—— asking for a catalogue and price list.
    I have pleasure in sending you a copy of the catalogue which gives all the prices, and an order form. We give 15% discount on orders of £150 or more, and payment must be made within 30 days of the date of the invoice. We send small orders within a week of receiving the order.
    We shall be very pleased if you decide to buy our goods,* and look forward to hearing from you.

Yours sincerely,

K. Drummond

K. Drummond
Sales Manager

Usually the catalogue and price lists will give all the information about discount, time of delivery and any other details that are necessary, but in order to make it quite clear Mr Drummond, the Sales Manager, has written all this in his letter to Mr Schoenenberger. He does this so that he can give Mr Schoenenberger the feeling that this is a personal letter and not just a formal one.

Here are some more letters of enquiry and replies to them:

Via S. Teresa no. 23,
689 Roma, Italia

Alberghi Motel Riuniti S.r.l.

The Manager,
Royal Grosvenor Porcelain Co., Ltd.,
Grosvenor House,
Renfrew Road,
Oakley,
Staffordshire,
England OA7 9AH   7th March 19——

Dear Sir,

We are refitting a number of the hotels in our group, and are interested in your china.

Please send me a complete catalogue and price list of all the types of china suitable for our use which you have available.* If your prices are reasonable,* and if you can deliver within eight weeks, we shall order sufficient for 3,000 guests. Please give your terms of business.

I shall look forward to hearing from you.

Yours faithfully,

Benedetto Brambilla

Benedetto Brambilla
Managing Director

This is a short way of asking for the information. Another way of writing the second paragraph is :

> Please send me a complete catalogue and price list of your best quality china which would be suitable for use in our internationally-known luxury hotels.

This is a more specific enquiry about china for a particular type of hotel.

Grosvenor House,
Renfrew Road,
Oakley,
Staffordshire OA7 9AH

Tel: Oakley (743 069) 60591/2/3

Royal Grosvenor Porcelain Company Ltd.

14.3.19—

Signore Benedetto Brambilla,
Alberghi Motel Riuniti S.r.l.,
Via S. Teresa no. 23,
689 Rome,
Italy.

Dear Mr Brambilla,
Thank you for your letter of 7.3.19— enquiring about our china.
I am sending you a copy of our catalogue and a current* price list. Our normal terms are 15% discount for large orders and also 12% for payment within thirty days; complete payment must be made in three months or less.
Our representative will be in Rome next month. If you can see him then, he will explain anything you do not understand. If you need any more information before then, please write and ask me.

Yours sincerely,

L. Sutherland
Sales Manager

If Mr Brambilla likes something in the catalogue he will probably want to know more about it. He would usually write and ask for more information, but since a representative of this firm is coming to Rome, Mr Brambilla can ask him when he arrives.

Via S. Teresa no. 23,
689 Roma, Italia

Alberghi Motel Riuniti S.r.l.

MZ/VF/7540

Mr L. Sutherland,
Sales Manager,
Royal Grosvenor Porcelain Co., Ltd.,
Grosvenor House,
Renfrew Road,
Oakley,
Staffordshire,
England OA7 9AH   19th March 19—

Dear Mr Sutherland,

Thank you for your letter of 14th March and the catalogue you sent.

We have read your catalogue carefully and have decided that we would like to buy the 'Regent' range. We should like to see your representative and ask for further information about several things. Please let me know when he will be in Rome so that we can arrange to see him.

I shall look forward to hearing from you again.

Yours sincerely,

Benedetto Brambilla

Benedetto Brambilla
Managing Director

Here is the reply to this letter:

Grosvenor House,
Renfrew Road,
Oakley,
Staffordshire OA7 9AH

Tel: Oakley (743 069) 60591/2/3

Royal Grosvenor Porcelain Company Ltd.

25.3.19—

Your Ref: MZ/VF/7540*

Signore Benedetto Brambilla,
Alberghi Motel Riuniti S.r.l.,
Via S. Teresa no. 23,
689 Rome,
Italy.

Dear Mr Brambilla,
   Thank you for your letter of 19th March.
   Mr Walker will be in Rome from 14th–18th April
inclusive, and will call to see you at any time which is
convenient.
   I hope he will be able to help you and that we shall
receive an order from you soon.

Yours sincerely,

L. Sutherland
Sales Manager

Via S. Teresa no. 23,
689 Roma, Italia

Alberghi Motel Riuniti S.r.l.

Mr L. Sutherland,
Sales Manager,
Royal Grosvenor Porcelain Co., Ltd.,
Grosvenor House,
Renfrew Road,
Oakley,
Staffordshire,
England OA7 9AH   30th March 19—

Dear Mr Sutherland,

Thank you for your letter of 25th March.

We would like to see Mr Walker at 11.00 on Wednesday,
15th April.

Yours sincerely,

Benedetto Brambilla

Benedetto Brambilla
Managing Director

Mr L. Sutherland,
Sales Manager,
Royal Grosvenor Porcelain Co., Ltd.,
Grosvenor House,
Renfrew Road,
Oakley,
Staffordshire,
England OA7 9AH

Note: This letter does not need a closing paragraph.

The Risborough Gallery

95 Thornton Hill,
Laxby,
Boxshire LA16 8VB

Tel: Lents Hill (0914) 01552

19th May 19—

The Export Manager,
Soderbergs Stal A.B.,
Storgatan 18,
Nystad,
Sweden.

Dear Sir,
   We are very interested in the new type of cutlery shown in your catalogue.
   We are not able to send a representative to the 'Gracious House' Exhibition next month, but would like to see a member of your firm when he is in England. In the meantime I should be glad if you would send me a sample of each of the following designs: 'Speedway', 'Thistle' and 'Summer Haze', as I think they will sell here. Please let me know your terms of business.
   I look forward to hearing from you.

Yours faithfully,

Martin Collyer

Martin Collyer
Import Manager

Soderbergs Stal A.B.

STORGATAN 18, Nystad, Sweden. Nystad 3295 406

28th May 19—

Mr Martin Collyer,
Import Manager,
The Risborough Gallery,
95 Thornton Hill,
Laxby,
Boxshire,
England LA16 8VB

Dear Mr Collyer,
    Thank you for your letter of 19th May.
    I enclose a 'Speedway' fork, a 'Thistle' knife and a 'Summer Haze' spoon for you to see. I hope you like them and if you do, we can send you as many as you need. Our terms are 15% discount on all orders of over £1,000, and payment must be made within 60 days.
    Mr Gustav Jorgensen will be in England for the week beginning Monday, 2nd July, and he can call on you then. He will be staying at 'The Castle Hotel', Lamford, and he will telephone you to make an appointment to see you.
    I hope this gives you the information you need. Mr Jorgensen will be able to answer any other questions.

Yours sincerely,

Bjorg Svensson

Bjorg Svensson
Export Manager

Note: This letter needs four paragraphs because it deals with two main ideas, each of which needs a paragraph.

If you write as a person, not as an employee of a firm, your letter will look like this:

14th September 19––

The Sales Manager,
Midland Electric Co., Ltd.,
25 Trinity Place,
Mackstown,
England MA12 7QE

Dear Sir,
   My friend has a 'Diamond' electric toaster and I should also like one.
   Please could you send me a leaflet* about this toaster and tell me how much it would cost.
   Can I buy one in Italy, or will you send me one?

Yours faithfully,

Pio Bonetti

Pio Bonetti

---

or like this:

The Manager,
Tournament Sports Goods Limited,
26–30 Ravensdale Road,
Farrington,
M. Glam,
England CA49 3JM

Dear Sir,

When I was in England recently a friend lent me her Tournament tennis racquet. I liked it very much and would like to have one of my own.

I should be pleased if you could send me a leaflet about these racquets and a price list. Are there any sports shops in Sweden which stock these racquets?

I look forward to hearing from you soon.

Yours faithfully,

Gustav Jorgensen

Gustav Jorgensen

The reply will be exactly like the reply to an employee of a firm:

MIDLAND ELECTRIC COMPANY LTD.

25 Trinity Place,   Tel: Mackstown 0710
Mackstown MA12 7QE   VAT Registration No. 378 4569 23

JA/FV

23rd September 19––

Signore Pio Bonetti,
Viale S. Pieri no. 7,
00910 Turin,
Italy.

Dear Mr Bonetti,
    Thank you for your letter of 14th September.
    I am sorry that we no longer make the 'Diamond' electric toaster. We now have a newer model, the 'Sapphire' which gives much more heat, is easier to use and much easier to clean. You will see from the pictures in the enclosed leaflet that it comes in several colours, as well as in stainless steel like the 'Diamond'.
    We shall be pleased to send you one, as we have no agent in Italy; please add £2.50 to the price in the leaflet, for packing and postage by an International Money Order or by a cheque drawn on a bank in this country (your bank can arrange this).
    I hope to hear from you again soon.

                    Yours sincerely,

                    J. Adams

                    J. Adams
                    Sales Manager

When you are writing to enquire about how much you must pay for anything, you will need to know about insurance and the cost of sending goods. The most common arrangements are:

ex-works, ex-factory	This is the price at the factory. The buyer pays the cost of sending the goods.
f.o.b. (port of export named) = free on board	This is most common. It is the price for the goods to be put on to the ship at the port (f.o.b. DOVER).
f.o.b. (port of import named)	This is the price to the port. But it does not include insurance or unloading (f.o.b. PIRAEUS).
c.i.f. (place named) =cost, insurance and freight*	This includes all costs to the place named, including insurance (c.i.f. ROME).

So when Mr Brambilla asks Mr Sutherland about his china (p. 14), he would reply, for instance, that his prices are f.o.b. LIVERPOOL, meaning that Mr Brambilla would pay for the cost of getting the china from the Liverpool warehouse* to his hotel.

Becoming an Agent

An agent, or a firm of agents, acts for a firm or a group of firms, usually in buying or selling. Agents normally try to do one kind of thing only. For example, shipping agents will arrange for goods to be sent, usually by sea, from one country to another; they will arrange to send all the necessary documents.*

The most usual form of agency,* however, is concerned with getting goods from the manufacturer into the shops which will sell them to the customers in a particular area—that is, from the wholesaler* to the retailer.* For doing this, the agent may either receive a percentage of the price of the goods—a commission*—or he may receive a fee.* This is normally less expensive for a firm than sending a member of its own staff to a foreign country, and a native of any country will almost always know the market* better than a foreigner will.

Anybody who wishes to act as an agent will write to the Managing Director of the firm he wishes to represent*:

15th May 19—

The Managing Director,
Lowsons Agrochemicals Ltd.,
Shepston,
Cambridgeshire,
England EL9 6UI

Dear Sir,
   You have probably read about the attempts we are making to improve our agriculture in this country.
   We already represent three American makers of agricultural chemicals, but none of them make chemicals which would be as good for our crops as yours. We would, therefore, like to add your chemicals to those of the American firms we represent. We think they would sell very well here.
   At present we hold large stocks, and pay for them every month as we sell them. We would like to continue this arrangement.
   We look forward to hearing from you.

                              Yours faithfully,

                              M. Azad

                              M. Azad
                              Sales Manager

Or the Managing Director of Lowsons may already have written to offer an agency to Mr Azad:

12th May 19—

Mr M. Azad,
Sales Manager,
Teheran Chemical Products,
P.O. Box 422,
Teheran,
Iran.

Dear Mr Azad,
    We think we could sell far more of our well known chemical products in the Middle East* and we are therefore looking for an agent to represent us. We would like to offer you the sole agency* in the Middle East.
    I enclose a catalogue and export price list so that you can see the wide range of chemicals we make. You can also see that many of them will be useful in the Middle East, as they are particularly good for its crops and climate.
    We should like to pay you a commission of 15% of the invoice value of the orders you take; we would pay this quarterly.* We could supply you on consignment* but would prefer to pay on a commission basis. We will provide £1,000 for an advertising campaign.
    We look forward to hearing from you.

Yours sincerely,

H. J. Kahn
Managing Director

You will note that each of these letters has four paragraphs. This is because two main ideas appear in the letter: why an agency is needed, and how the agent is to be paid. Each separate idea gets a paragraph of its own – even if it is only one sentence.

A letter is then written to confirm the details:

Mr M. Azad,
Sales Manager,
Teheran Chemical Products,
P.O. Box 422,
Teheran,
Iran.   30th May 19——

Dear Mr Azad,
   Thank you for your letter of 21st May about the Middle East Agency.
   These are the points we have agreed on:
1. You will operate as* our sole agents in the Middle East.
2. You will receive a commission of 15% of the invoice value on all the orders you get.
3. You will be paid quarterly and will send your account two weeks before payment must be made.
4. You will send us your proposals for an advertising campaign; we agree to pay £1,000 towards its cost.
5. We shall consider the arrangements again every 18 months.
   Please let me know if you agree with these points. If so, I shall send you a draft agreement for your signature.

                        Yours sincerely,

                        H. J. Kahn

                        H. J. Kahn
                        Managing Director

Exercises

Note: When you ask the price of something, you should say how you will pay for insurance and for freight.

1 You have seen the catalogue of Longlen Products Ltd., 831 Northern Road, Bourn, Oxford OX1 8ZF, which makes a particular kind of product your firm uses. (For example, you may be interested in parts which are used in making your product, such as leather, thread, etc.).

(a) Who would you write to for information? Begin and end your letter, including the firm's address.

(b) Start a letter explaining what you have seen and where.

(c) Explain what you would like to know.

(d) Explain what you would like your correspondent to do.

(e) Now imagine that you have seen a catalogue for the products of Leinster Company Limited, 82 Footden Road, London N31 6KR. This firm makes another product you are interested in. Write a letter asking for more information about it.

2 You have received a reply from the Sales Manager, Mr F. White, of Longlen Products. He explains that he has a wide range of the particular product which interests you, that the price varies from £110.75 per hundred to £262.50 per hundred, and if you tell him more about what you are going to use the product for, he will advise you which will be the best for you.

(a) Begin and end his letter, including the firm's address.

(b) What will he say in the first paragraph? How many sentences will he use? Write the paragraph.

(c) How much of the information in the question would he use in his second paragraph? Write this yourself.

(d) What will he say in the third paragraph? In how many sentences? Write the third paragraph.

(e) Now write out the complete letter.

3 Your name is Harold Jones, Manager of Electronics Ltd., 3 Stockbridge Road, Liverpool LP5 2OM. You have seen a portable colour television set, the Hoyo 153, in a shop in London. It is manufactured by the Fuji Company with offices at 153 Ginza-chome, Tokyo, Japan, and it sells for £202. This is better and cheaper than anything else you have seen, and you would like to stock these in your shop.

(a) Write to the Fuji Company to find out about the possibility of buying this set. Mention how many you expect to sell in a year, and ask for the terms of business and the delivery dates.*

(b) Mr Hashimoto, the Sales Manager of Fuji, replies to your letter. He explains that the wholesale* price, for orders of 50 or more, is £170 each, that this already includes a discount of over 15%, and that there is a further 10% discount if payment is made within 30 days. All the money due must be paid within 3 months. He sends the goods as soon as he receives the order, usually the same day. Write Mr Hashimoto's letter.

(c) Because of the distance from Japan to England, the goods will take a long time (6–12 weeks) to arrive. Answer letter (b), explaining this, and saying that you need more time to pay. Ask if he can give you more time or better terms.

(d) You are Mr Hashimoto. Write and say that you will give 180 days' credit.*

(e) Write to an English company at 592 Lower Lane, Birmingham BI76 3RN, making the same enquiry about a product your firm is interested in.

4 You are the Sales Manager of a firm in your own country. You have seen samples of a product you are interested in at an exhibition in your own country. Write to the English firm exhibiting there, at 168 Elsenham Street, Luton, Beds LU49 3MA, and ask for more information. (Do not forget to explain where you saw them and to end with a paragraph explaining that you are waiting to hear from the firm you are writing to.)

5 Imagine that Mr T. Smith, of The Midland Company Ltd., 139 Lower Street, Coventry, West Midlands CO2 9CZ, has written the letter in Exercise 4 to you, as Sales Manager of a firm in your country. Answer this letter.

6 Write to ask if you can act as an agent for the International Caravan Group, Hales Road, Newmarket, Suffolk CB29 5DO in your country. Explain how you would like to be paid.

7 You are the Sales Manager of British Sports Cars Limited, and feel that you would like to increase your sales in America. Write to Mr J. L. Smith, 1938 Plains Avenue, Orangewood, New Jersey 18695421 offering him the agency at 25% commission. Explain how you will pay him and when you will think about changing the arrangement and how often. Are you going to suggest he advertises your cars? If so, explain how much you will pay towards the cost of this.

3. Orders and Complaints

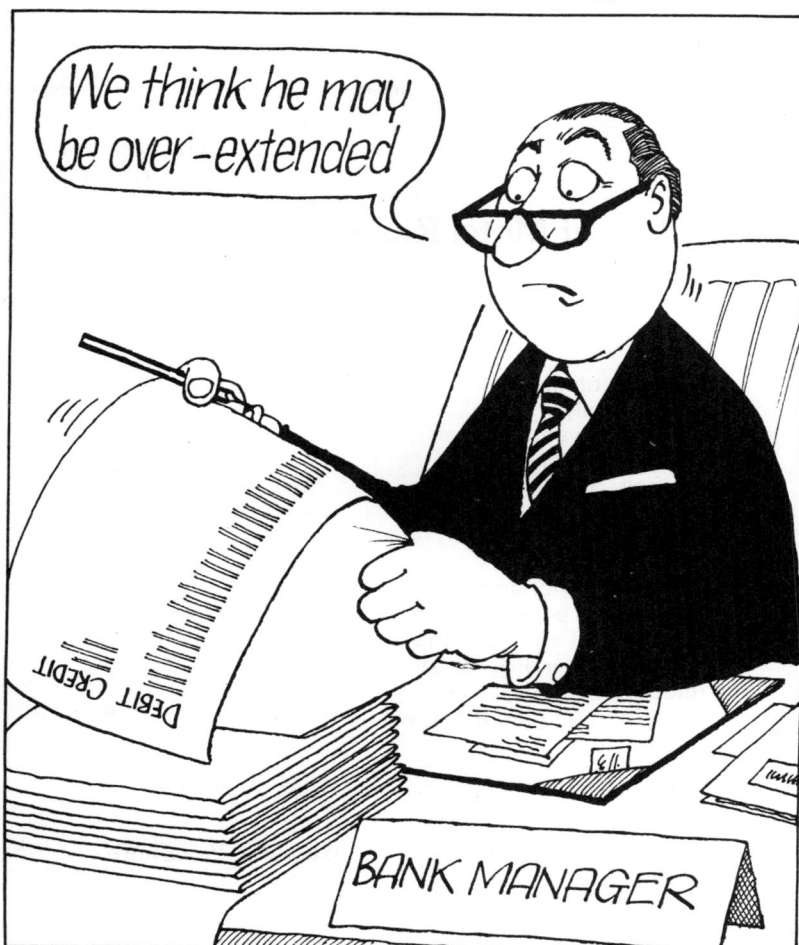

If you have found something which you would like to buy, you will need to write and order it. In England, many companies have printed forms* for this, but you can also order something by writing a letter. Before a firm will send you anything, it will normally ask you to give two references to show that you pay what you owe promptly. One of these references will usually be a bank, and the other a firm known to both of you and from whom you have already bought something.

If an English firm wishes to buy some of your firm's products, you will need to ask for its references in the same way.
An order may be sent with a letter:

Via S. Teresa no. 23,
689 Roma, Italia

Alberghi Motel Riuniti S.r.l.

16th April 19—

Mr L. Sutherland,
Sales Manager,
Royal Grosvenor Porcelain Co., Ltd.,
Grosvenor House,
Renfrew Road,
Oakley,
Staffordshire OA7 9AH

Dear Mr Sutherland,
I was very pleased to meet Mr Walker yesterday. He was very helpful and gave me all the information I needed.
I enclose our order and hope to receive the china by the middle of June.
I should be glad if you would let me know when the order is sent.

Yours sincerely,

Benedetto Brambilla

Benedetto Brambilla
Managing Director

The reply would begin:

Thank you for your letter of 16th April 19—, containing your order . . . .

Or the order may have been taken by a representative or agent. The reply, asking for references, will be:

Grosvenor House,
Renfrew Road,
Oakley,
Staffordshire OA7 9AH

Tel: Oakley (743 069) 60591/2/3

Royal Grosvenor Porcelain Company Ltd.

30.4.19—

Signore Benedetto Brambilla,
Managing Director,
Alberghi Motel Riuniti S.r.l.,
Via S. Teresa no. 23,
689 Rome,
Italy.

Dear Mr Brambilla,
    We were very pleased to hear from Mr Walker that you have placed a large order with us.
    Before we can send the goods we must ask you for the usual references: one from your bank and one from another firm from whom you have bought goods. I would be glad if you would let me have the names and addresses as soon as possible so that I may write to them. These references will, of course, be treated as private* and confidential.
    I look forward to hearing from you again soon.

Yours sincerely,

L. Sutherland
Sales Manager

32

Here is the answer to this letter:

Via S. Teresa no. 23,
689 Roma, Italia

Alberghi Motel Riuniti S.r.l.

MZ/DK/7540

Mr L. Sutherland,
Sales Manager,
Royal Grosvenor Porcelain Co., Ltd.,
Grosvenor House,
Renfrew Road,
Oakley,
Staffordshire,
England OA7 9AH   5th May 19—

Dear Mr Sutherland,

Thank you for your letter of 30th April.

We bank with the Banco Milano, Viale S. Roberto 109,
Rome, and we have recently bought carpets from The
Colourfloor Co., Ltd., of 238 Wilton Road, Axminster,
England AX2 1AS. Both the bank and The Colourfloor Co.,
Ltd. will be able to supply references.

I hope these will be satisfactory and that we shall receive
our china as soon as possible.

Yours sincerely,

Benedetto Brambilla

Benedetto Brambilla
Managing Director

As the order on p. 31 was given to Mr Walker, he made sure he had all the details. Goods can, of course, be ordered on a special order form (usually sent with the catalogue), or by writing a letter. Make sure you give all the information needed, and that all the details are correct and you order exactly what you want.

Note: In England and America a full stop (.) and not a comma (,) is used for the decimal point. A comma is used to separate thousands and hundreds, e.g. 21,269 *not* 21.269, which in England or America would be 21 and 269 thousandths.

Here is another example of an order. The order is sent on a form, and this is the letter which explains it:

ODYSSEUS HOTEL

Xanthi Str., Athens, Greece

The Sales Manager,
Byfords Foods Ltd.,
Optimax House,
Marsden Road,
Moulton,
Cheshire,
England MO14 9KG   6th March 19——

Dear Sir,
    Thank you for sending your catalogue and price list.
    I enclose the order form and would be grateful if you would send the goods as soon as possible. I should like to claim the trade discount* and intend to pay within 30 days.
    I look forward to receiving the order.

Yours faithfully,

F. Loscher.

F. Loscher
Manager

Note: Either 'would' or 'should' can be used; the difference between them is disappearing in modern English, especially in spoken English.

Here is the order form:

ODYSSEUS HOTEL

Xanthi Str., Athens, Greece

To: **Byfords Foods Limited,**
Optimax House,
Marsden Road,
Moulton,
Cheshire MO14 9KG

PURCHASE ORDER
No. 256/B/22/JK

Date 6th March 19—

Please supply the following

Quantity	Description		Price £	P
5	931 A		31	00
10	952 C		175	00
20	1061 A		80	00
10	52 B		100	00
20	824 B		110	00
30	1206 C		450	00
			946	00

Date delivery required	Delivery address	For Odysseus Hotel Limited
As soon as possible	**Odysseus Hotel,** **Xanthi Str.,** **Athens,** **Greece.**	Signed *F. Loscher.*

The abbreviation 'No.' is explained in the glossary.

(The invoice for this order is found on p. 48.)

Note: The reference number, 256/B/22/JK, is important (exactly as it would be in the letter), because it helps the reader to find any earlier letters about this order.

It is, of course, possible to give an order in a letter and not on a form. Mr Brambilla might give an order to Mr Sutherland in this way:

Via S. Teresa no. 23,
689 Roma, Italia

Alberghi Motel Riuniti S.r.l.

19th March 19—

Mr L. Sutherland,
Sales Manager,
Royal Grosvenor Porcelain Co., Ltd.,
Grosvenor House,
Renfrew Road,
Oakley,
Staffordshire,
England OA7 9AH

Dear Mr Sutherland,

Thank you for your letter of 14th March and the catalogue you sent.

We should like to buy 3,000 plates in both sizes and 3,000 cups and saucers of the Regent range.

We should be glad if you would let us know when these goods are despatched.*

Yours sincerely,

Benedetto Brambilla

Benedetto Brambilla
Managing Director

When Mr Brambilla receives Mr Sutherland's letter asking for references he will reply, giving them (see p. 32).

Mr Sutherland will have to ask his bank to write to his customer's banker, as banks will not give any information about a client's financial affairs except to another bank:

Grosvenor House,
Renfrew Road,
Oakley,
Staffordshire OA7 9AH

Tel: Oakley (743 069) 60591/2/3

Royal Grosvenor Porcelain Company Ltd.

The Manager,
The Commercial Bank Ltd.,
Grange Branch,
181 High Street,
Oakley,
Staffordshire OA1 2LX   10.5.19—

Dear Sir,
   We have received a large order from a new customer in
Italy for goods amounting to £7,000.
   The firm is Allerghi Motel Riuniti S.r.l. of Via S. Teresa
no. 23, 689 Rome, Italy and they bank with Banco Milano,
Viale S. Roberto 109, Rome. We would be grateful if you
could make enquiries on our behalf.
   I hope to hear from you soon.

Yours faithfully,

L. Sutherland
Sales Manager

When the bank replies, it will not give any details but will
say that it has heard from Banco Milano 'who consider you
would be safe to allow Alberghi Motel Riuniti S.r.l. credit for
the amount you mentioned'. This means that the bank
believes the firm is reliable and will pay its bills. If the reply
says that the bank 'regrets it is unable to give any information
about the firm', it means that the bank does not think it is safe
to allow the firm this amount of credit. If it says that a firm will
be 'over-extended' by being allowed credit for a certain
amount, it means that the firm is reliable but that it is only safe
for a smaller amount than you mention.

A firm may be able to give more information, particularly about its own dealings with another business. Both the bank and the firm to which you have written for references will probably say that the information is given 'without responsibility'. This means that the information given is as accurate as possible, but it may not be correct. The giver of the information will not accept blame if it is inaccurate, and will not repay any money lost because of incorrect information.

If you are asking a firm to do something for you, it is normal to pay them the cost of the postage. This is done by enclosing a stamped addressed envelope, sometimes shortened to s.a.e.*

Here is a reply from Mr Sutherland's bank:

The Commercial Bank Limited
Grange Branch

181 High Street,
Oakley,
Staffordshire OA1 2LX

PRIVATE AND CONFIDENTIAL
RW/BM   20th May 19—
Mr L. Sutherland,
Sales Manager,
Royal Grosvenor Porcelain Co., Ltd.,
Grosvenor House,
Renfrew Road,
Oakley,
Staffordshire OA7 9AH

Dear Sir,

Alberghi Motel Riuniti S.r.l.

Thank you for your letter of 10th May.

We have heard from Banco Milano in Rome, who consider you would be safe to allow Alberghi Motel Riuniti S.r.l. credit for the amount you mentioned. They say that this firm has banked with them for over ten years.

Their account is always in credit* and Banco Milano confirms that the firm is able to pay this amount.

Yours faithfully,

R. Wilkinson
Manager

38

If the bank does not think Alberghi Motel Riuniti S.r.l. would be able to pay this amount, Mr Sutherland would receive a letter like this:

The Commercial Bank Limited
Grange Branch

181 High Street,
Oakley,
Staffordshire OA1 2LX

PRIVATE AND CONFIDENTIAL

RW/BM   20th May 19—

Mr L. Sutherland,
Sales Manager,
Royal Grosvenor Porcelain Co., Ltd.,
Grosvenor House,
Renfrew Road,
Oakley,
Staffordshire OA7 9AH

Dear Mr Sutherland,

Thank you for your letter of 10th May.

We have been in touch with the Banco Milano, Rome. They tell us they think Alberghi Motel Riuniti S.r.l. would be over-extended by being allowed a credit for the amount you mention.

Yours sincerely,

R. Wilkinson
Manager

Note: This letter is written to 'Dear Mr Sutherland' and ends 'Yours sincerely'. It is probable that Mr Sutherland and his business are well known to the bank.

Here is a letter asking for a business reference:

Grosvenor House,
Renfrew Road,
Oakley,
Staffordshire OA7 9AH

Tel: Oakley (743 069) 60591/2/3

Royal Grosvenor Porcelain Company Ltd.

10.5.19—

PRIVATE AND CONFIDENTIAL

The Manager,
The Colourfloor Co., Ltd.,
238 Wilton Road,
Axminster AX2 1AS

Dear Sir,
 I understand from Mr Benedetto Brambilla, the
Managing Director of Alberghi Motel Riuniti S.r.l. of
Rome, that he has recently transacted* business with you.
He now wants to place an order with us. The sum involved
will be about £7,000 and I should be grateful if you would
let me know if you consider him credit-worthy* for this
amount.
 I enclose a stamped addressed envelope for your reply.

Yours faithfully,

L. Sutherland
Sales Manager

Here is a possible reply:

The Colourfloor Company Ltd.

238 Wilton Road,
Axminster,
England AX2 1AS

15.5.19—

PRIVATE AND CONFIDENTIAL

Mr L. Sutherland,
Sales Manager,
Royal Grosvenor Porcelain Co., Ltd.,
Grosvenor House,
Renfrew Road,
Oakley,
Staffordshire OA7 9AH

Dear Mr Sutherland,
    Thank you for your letter of 10.5.19—.
    Alberghi Motel Riuniti S.r.l. have an account with us.
They recently placed a very large order with us; they paid
the full amount promptly, and they have always done so
in the past. We consider them to be a very reliable firm.
    Of course, this information is given without
responsibility.

Yours sincerely,

K. J. Long
Manager

Or they may reply:

The Colourfloor Company Ltd.

238 Wilton Road,
Axminster,
England AX2 1AS

15.5.19—

PRIVATE AND CONFIDENTIAL

Mr. L. Sutherland,
Sales Manager,
Royal Grosvenor Porcelain Co., Ltd.,
Renfrew Road,
Oakley,
Staffordshire OA7 9AH

Dear Mr Sutherland,

   Alberghi Motel Riuniti S.r.l.

Thank you for your letter of 10.5.19—.

We have had only one order from Alberghi Motel Riuniti
S.r.l., so we regret we cannot give you a reference from
long experience. We had some difficulty in getting our
money.

This information is given without responsibility.

Yours sincerely,

K. J. Long
Manager

If the replies are satisfactory, an order can be accepted:

Grosvenor House,
Renfrew Road,
Oakley,
Staffordshire OA7 9AH

Tel: Oakley (743 069) 60591/2/3

Royal Grosvenor Porcelain Company Ltd.

20th May 19—

Signore Benedetto Brambilla,
Alberghi Motel Riuniti S.r.l.,
Via S. Teresa no. 23,
689 Rome,
Italy.

Dear Mr Brambilla,
    Thank you for your letter of 5th May giving the names of two references.
    Your order for 3,000 'Regent' plates in two sizes, cups and saucers has been despatched today. The necessary documents are being sent under separate cover.*
    I hope you will be pleased with this china and that we shall do more business with you.

Yours sincerely,

L. Sutherland
Sales Manager

Note: Many firms have printed 'Receipt of order' forms which are sent to the buyer. Futher information about documents will be found in Chapter 4, dealing with methods of payment.

Mr Brambilla may be very pleased with the goods he has received, and if so, he might write and say so:

Via S. Teresa no. 23,
689 Roma, Italia

Alberghi Motel Riuniti S.r.l.

13th June 19——

Mr L. Sutherland,
Sales Manager,
Royal Grosvenor Porcelain Co., Ltd.,
Grosvenor House,
Renfrew Road,
Oakley,
Staffordshire,
England OA7 9AH

Dear Mr Sutherland,
   Thank you for the china.
   We are delighted with it and would like to congratulate you on its excellent quality and for the way it was packed. Not a single item was broken in transit.*
   We will certainly recommend your china to other people in the hotel business.

Yours sincerely,

Benedetto Brambilla

Benedetto Brambilla
Managing Director

It is polite to write a short reply to a letter like this (see next page).

Grosvenor House,
Renfrew Road,
Oakley,
Staffordshire OA7 9AH

Tel: Oakley (743 069) 60591/2/3

Royal Grosvenor Porcelain Company Ltd.

17th June 19—

Signore Benedetto Brambilla,
Alberghi Motel Riuniti S.r.l.,
Via S. Teresa no. 23,
689 Rome,
Italy.

Dear Mr Brambilla,
   Thank you for your letter of 13th June.
   I am very glad to know that you are pleased with the 'Regent' china.
   I am delighted that you will recommend our china to other hotel owners.

Yours sincerely,

L. Sutherland
Sales Manager

If Mr Brambilla has a complaint to make he will write to Mr Sutherland telling him what is wrong.

If the complaint is justified, the firm will write and say so and will either replace the faulty items, or will give him a credit* or a refund* for their price. The firm will probably ask him to return any faulty items.

Via S. Teresa no. 23,
689 Roma, Italia

Alberghi Motel Riuniti S.r.l.

Mr L. Sutherland,
Sales Manager,
Royal Grosvenor Porcelain Co., Ltd.,
Grosvenor House,
Renfrew Road,
Oakley,
Staffordshire,
England OA7 9AH   29th June 19—

Dear Mr Sutherland,

Thank you for the china which arrived later than you promised.

We are pleased with the quality but the packing was not very good. Twelve (12) large plates, five (5) small plates, fifteen (15) cups and three (3) saucers were broken. We should be grateful if you would send replacements immediately.

Yours sincerely,

Benedetto Brambilla

Benedetto Brambilla
Managing Director

You will see that the quantity is given in figures as well as words, for example 'Twelve (12) large plates, five (5), small plates . . .'. Whenever the actual number of items is important (usually in connection with quantities in an order, or amounts of money), it is better to use both figures and words. Figures must always be used, even if words are not. But it is better to use both, so there can be no room for misunderstanding.

Mr Brambilla would hope to get an answer like this:

Grosvenor House,
Renfrew Road,
Oakley,
Staffordshire OA7 9AH

Tel: Oakley (743 069) 60591/2/3

Royal Grosvenor Porcelain Company Ltd.

3rd July 19—

Signore Benedetto Brambilla,
Alberghi Motel Riuniti S.r.l.,
Via S. Teresa no. 23,
689 Rome,
Italy.

Dear Mr Brambilla,

Thank you for your letter of 29th June.

I am very sorry so many items of the 'Regent' china were found to be broken on arrival. I have already asked the warehouse and the shippers to look into this matter so that it will not happen again. I have sent replacements for the broken pieces today and I hope they will reach you in good condition within two weeks.

Please accept my apologies for any inconvenience this has caused you. Would you please return the broken items so that we can claim from our insurance company.

Yours sincerely,

L. Sutherland
Sales Manager

Exercises

1 You wish to place an order for 15 men's bicycles, 15 ladies' bicycles, 15 boys' bicycles and 15 girls' bicycles, from the Drake Manufacturing Company, 153 Gilbert Road, Southampton, England SO19 1QA. The prices of these are: £36.50, £34.75, £22.15 and £21.15.

(a) Write and order them.

(b) You are Mr H. Green, the Sales Manager of the Drake Manufacturing Company. Answer the last letter, asking for two references.

(c) You are Mr Green. Write a letter to each of these references, asking about the reliability of your customer. (Use a bank and a firm in your own country for the names and addresses.)

(d) Write a favourable reply from a bank in your own country.

(e) Write a favourable reply from a firm in your own country.

2 If you read in a letter of reference from a bank: 'We regret we can give you no information about this firm', what does it mean? How would the bank write if it recommended the firm?

3 What would it mean if, in a letter of reference, you read:

(a) '. . . we feel they may be over-extended.'

(b) '. . . we have had only one order from them and they paid for it promptly.'

(c) '. . . we have dealt with this company for some years, but we have always had some delays in obtaining payment.'

(d) Would you be happy to open an account in the case of (a), (b), and (c)? Why (or why not)?

4 You have received the bicycles you ordered in Exercise 1. You are very annoyed to find that they were badly packed, and that 12 of the men's bicycles were badly scratched.

(a) Write to Mr Green and complain.

(b) Give Mr Green's answer to your letter.

5 The bicycles you ordered in Exercise 1 are so very good that you have sold them all. Write and say how pleased you are, and order again, asking for twice as many as before.

4. Payment

The cases must be labelled so that they are easy to find.
When you receive the goods you have ordered you will receive
an invoice. This usually looks like this:

Byfords Foods Ltd.

Optimax House, Marsden Road,
Moulton, Cheshire MO14 9KG

Tel: Moulton (0599) 8631/2/3
Telex: 23 1426 80

VAT Reg. No. 4621 40 720

Odysseus Hotel,
Xanthi Str.,
Athens,
Greece.

10th March 19—

INVOICE No. 60136

Your order no. 256/B/22/JK

Cat. no.	Size	Quantity	Price	£
931	A	5	6.20	31.00
952	C	10	17.50	175.00
1061	A	20	4.00	80.00
52	B	10	10.00	100.00
824	B	20	5.50	110.00
1206	C	30	15.00	450.00
				946.00
			Less 5% trade discount	47.30
				898.70
			Packing	15.00
Terms 90 days 5%				913.70
M/V Silver Star				
4 cases				
BYFL 76/AX				

The abbreviation 'M/V' is explained in the Glossary.

As you can see, an invoice gives a lot of information.

The first thing it tells you is who is sending the goods, to whom and when:

Byfords Foods Ltd.

Optimax House, Marsden Road,
Moulton, Cheshire MO14 9KG

Tel: Moulton (0599) 8631/2/3
Telex: 23 1426 80

VAT Reg. No. 4621 40 720

10th March 19—

• The invoice number lets the firm look it up quickly if there is any question about it later on:

INVOICE No. 60136

There is a reference to your order, so that you can refer to it quickly if you need to. If you use a printed form, the reference will probably be a number; if your order was in a letter, it will give the date of your letter:

Your order no. 256/B/22/JK

Your letter of 16th March 19--

The columns tell you what is being ordered, how many (or how much) of it, the price of each thing which is being ordered, and the total cost:

Cat. no.	Size	Quantity	Price	£
(refers to the catalogue number of the item)		(how many)	(of each item)	(total cost)
931	A	5	6.20	31.00
952	C	10	17.50	175.00
1061	A	20	4.00	80.00
52	B	10	10.00	100.00
824	B	20	5.50	110.00
1206	C	30	15.00	450.00
				946.00

Because you are a firm ordering from another firm, you need not pay the full price, and you will get a certain reduction for ordering a large quantity (the amount depends on the terms of business explained in Chapter 2). This is often called a trade discount, and this is how it appears on the invoice:

```
Less 5%
trade discount
```

The terms of business include a reduction for prompt payment, and this is shown on the invoice. (If you pay quickly enough to earn this, you will subtract it from the total when you pay.)

```
Terms 90 days 5%
```

If special packing is required, it is usually charged for:

```
Packing
```

The invoice also gives information about the way in which the goods are sent (usually by sea, sometimes by air freight), and enough information to identify the cases in which they are packed. (This is useful for identifying the goods when they arrive and for clearing them through Customs.)

```
M/V Silver Star
4 Cases
BYFL 76/AX
```

So the invoice gives a great deal of information. Its main purpose, of course, is to explain how much the goods cost; but in doing this, it also describes the goods, how they are being sent, and to whom; and it gives some information about the sender by describing his terms of business.

In some ways the invoice is the most important document in any business transaction, and copies of it are used by the warehouse, the accounts department, the sales department and – in some firms – the production department.

If there is anything in the invoice you do not understand, you can write and ask about it:

The Sales Manager,
Byfords Foods Ltd.,
Optimax House,
Marsden Road,
Moulton,
Cheshire,
England MO14 9KG   14th March 19—

Dear Sir,
    Thank you for sending the invoice, No. 60136.
    I am surprised that item 1061, size A, costs £4.00. The price list you sent me gives the price as £3.80. Would you please explain this.
    I look forward to hearing from you.

Yours faithfully,

F. Loscher

F. Loscher
Manager

You will soon receive a reply:

---

20 March 19—

Dear Mr Loscher,
    Thank you for your letter of 14th March.
    I must apologize: you have a copy of last year's price list. We have had to increase the price because of the increased cost of the ingredients, and item 1061 is now £4.00.
    However, we shall of course charge you the old price. I therefore enclose a credit note for £4.00, which is the difference. I am sorry for the mistake.

Yours sincerely,

T. Brown

T. Brown
Manager

A Credit Note (C/N) is used if too much has been charged for something. It is always printed in red, and looks like this:

Credit by

Byfords Foods Ltd.

Optimax House, Marsden Road,
Moulton, Cheshire MO14 9KG

Tel: Moulton (0599) 8631/2/3
Telex: 23 1426 80

VAT Reg. No. 4621 40 720

Odysseus Hotel,
Xanthi Str.,
Athens,
Greece.

20th March 19—

CREDIT NOTE No. 103

Your order no.	Description	£	p
256/B/22/JK	To overcharging: 20 1061 A @ £0.20 With apologies	4	00

The sign @ is explained in the Glossary.

If you have been charged too little, a Debit Note, showing how much more you must pay, is sent. It is not printed in red and refers to 'Debit' (not 'Credit').

DEBIT

To undercharging on our Invoice no. 60136

Item 52B charged	£100
should have been	£110
	£10

With apologies

You may send several orders in a period of three months, and you may prefer to pay for them all together. In this case, you will receive a Statement of Account. (This arrangement is called an Open Account.)

A Statement of Account can be written in several ways, but the most common is the debit/credit and balance⋆ type:

Byfords Foods Ltd.

Optimax House, Marsden Road,
Moulton, Cheshire MO14 9KG

Tel: Moulton (0599) 8631/2/3
Telex: 23 1426 80

VAT Reg. No. 4621 40 720

Odysseus Hotel,
Xanthi Str.,
Athens,
Greece.

July 19—

STATEMENT

Date	Ref. no. (invoice, C/N or D/N)	Debit	Credit	Balance
1.3.19—	49037	739.56		739.56
10.3.19—	60136	913.70		1,653.26
20.3.19—	CN 103		4.00	1,649.26
12.6.19—	93921	866.79		2,516.05
		TERMS 90 DAYS	AMOUNT DUE ➡	2,516.05

The last amount shown in the 'Balance' column is the amount which has to be paid.

Many large firms have to start preparing the Statements of Account before the end of the quarter, so the body of the statement may look like this:

Balance carried forward				1,943.78
1.3.19—	49037	739.56		2,683.34
28.2.19—			1,943.78	739.56
10.3.19—	60136	913.70		1,653.26
20.3.19—	CN 103		4.00	1,649.26
12.6.19—	93921	866.79		2,516.05

'Balance carried forward' is explained in the Glossary.

This shows that on 28th February the Odysseus Hotel owed Byfords Foods Limited the sum of £1,943.78; when it was paid this was shown in the credit column.

You may need to ask for a Pro Forma invoice so that you can get permission to send money out of your country. This is an ordinary invoice with the words 'Pro Forma' printed across it, and it is exactly the same as the invoice you will receive when the goods are sent. It also means that you must send the money before the goods are despatched. A Pro Forma invoice is also very useful for the buyer, as he can find out exactly how much he must pay for the goods.

Byfords Foods Ltd.

Optimax House, Marsden Road,
Moulton, Cheshire MO14 9KG

Tel: Moulton (0599) 8631/2/3
Telex: 23 1426 80

VAT Reg. No. 4621 40 720

Odysseus Hotel,
Xanthi Str.,
Athens,
Greece.

10th March 19—

INVOICE No. 60136

Your order no. 256/B/22/JK

Cat. no.	Size	Quantity	Price	£
931	A	5	6.20	31.00
952	C	10	17.50	175.00
1061	A	20	4.00	80.00
52	B	10	10.00	100.00
824	B	20	5.50	110.00
1206	C	30	15.00	450.00
				946.00
			Less 5% trade discount	47.30
				898.70
			Packing	15.00
Terms 90 days 5% M/V Silver Star 4 cases BYFL 76/AX				913.70

The most common way of paying in international trade is the Bill of Exchange (B/E). This is an order telling you to pay a sum of money, and is sent by the firm supplying the goods. You agree to do this by signing your name across the front of it, or *accepting* it. It can be made payable *at sight* (on the day it is given to the seller), or at 30, 60 or 90 days *after sight* (30 d/s, 60 d/s, 90 d/s), so that you do not pay until you receive the goods, or for some time afterwards. There are usually three copies of each Bill, in case one or two get lost, but only the first copy to be accepted is used; the others are worth nothing after one has been signed.

Oakley 4th June 19—   £7,000.00

At Thirty days after Sight Pay to our Order the sum
Seven Thousand Pounds Sterling.

Value received

Accepted payable at Banco Milano Rome pp. Alberghi Motel Benedetto Brambilla Managing Director

To: Alberghi Motel Riuniti S.r.l.,
Via S. Teresa no. 23,
689 Rome, Italy.

Signed **M. Windsor**
Royal Grosvenor Porcelain Co. Ltd.
Oakley.

A Documentary Bill of Exchange guarantees payment. It is given to the bank with the shipping documents, the insurance policy, and the invoice, and the bank will give them to you when it receives your payment.

You can pay by a Letter of Credit (L/C). Your bank will arrange to have money available at a bank in London. An *irrevocable* Letter of Credit cannot be cancelled, and the seller of the goods then knows for certain that he will be paid. These letters are usually used when a firm is dealing with a customer for the first time, before he has opened an account.

TELEPHONE NUMBER: 68493/4/5   CABLES & TELEGRAMS: MILANOBANK ROME

BANCO MILANO
Foreign Department

Royal Grosvenor Porcelain Co. Ltd.,
Grosvenor House,
Renfrew Road,
Oakley,
Staffordshire OA7 9AH

ROME **10 JUNE 19—** 19......
Italy
This credit is advised to you through:

Banco Milano,
68 East Street,
London EC2.

With whom all correspondence
should be conducted.

IRREVOCABLE CONFIRMED CREDIT
No. LON/320/48/821

DEAR SIR(S),

We have pleasure in advising you that we have established this Irrevocable Credit
in your favour at the request of

Alberghi Motel Riuniti S.r.l., Via S. Teresa no. 23, 689 Rome, Italy

for the sum of £7,000 (Seven Thousand Pounds)

available by presentation for payment of your drafts drawn at Sight

on Alberghi Motel Riuniti S.r.l., Via S. Teresa no. 23, 689 Rome, Italy.

Negotiation is permitted in U.K. until 15.12.—

Yours faithfully,

B. di Palma.

for BANCO MILANO

A. Sidoti

for BANCO MILANO

Exercises

1 Here is an invoice:

Grosvenor House,
Renfrew Road,
Oakley,
Staffordshire OA7 9AH

Tel: Oakley (743 069) 60591/2/3

Royal Grosvenor Porcelain Company Ltd.

Alberghi Motel Riuniti S.r.l.,
Via S. Teresa no. 23,
689 Rome,
Italy.

INVOICE No. 9365B

20th May 19—

Your Order 19.3.19—

Quantity	Description & ref. no.	Style	Price	£
3,000	plates 821A	Regent	50p	1,500.00
3,000	plates 821B	"	60p	1,800.00
3,000	cups 967	"	75p	2,250.00
3,000	saucers 968	"	40p	1,200.00
				6,750.00
			Less 5% trade discount	337.50
M/V Prince Igor 10 cases				6,412.50
RGPCL HI.R/MZ	Terms 60 days 5%			

(a) Who is the buyer?
(b) Who is the seller?
(c) What is the trade discount?
(d) What are 'terms of business'?
(e) What is the meaning of the letters and figures in the lower left-hand corner of the invoice?

2 When would you use a Credit Note? Where has a C/N been used, and for how much, in the Statement on p. 53?

3 Why is a Documentary B/E a safeguard to the seller?

4 Explain when you would use a Bill of Exchange, and what it is. Why do you think it is not always paid at sight?

5 When would a British firm ask you to pay with an irrevocable L/C?

6 On checking the invoice in question (p. 57), you realize that you have been charged for 3,000 plates 821A, but have only received 2,000. Write and point this out to Mr Sutherland, the Sales Manager of the Royal Grosvenor Porcelain Company Ltd.

7 Rewrite the invoice, correcting the amounts as a result of this change.

8 You are Mr Sutherland. Write and apologize for the mistake.

5. Visiting England

You may come to England for your firm, and this chapter tells you some things which will help you when you arrive. (It includes booking hotels, making telephone calls and making appointments.)

Booking Hotels

You will need to book a room at a hotel. The letter you write will have, as usual, three main paragraphs. In the first, you explain what you are writing about:

```
The Manager,
The Hotel de Luxe,
Park Lane,
London W.1.,
England.                          15th January 19—
```

Dear Sir,
    I shall be staying in London. I shall arrive on Monday, 5th February and leave on Wednesday, 17th February.

A double-bedded room has one bed for two people; a twin-bedded room has two small (single) beds; a single room has one bed and is for one person. Most good hotels have a private bathroom with every room, but if you would like one you should say so:

> I should like to book a single room with private bath for this period.

In your last paragraph, you can ask about the price of the room. Most English hotels, but not all, provide breakfast and include it in the price of the room. You can ask about this, and also about any other charges (many hotels add 10–15% to the bill for service).

> I should be grateful if you would tell me how much it will cost, and if breakfast is included in the price. Are there any other charges?

You end, as usual: Yours faithfully,

You will note in this letter that you say exactly when you are going to arrive and leave. This avoids any chance of misunderstanding. You will also note that you ask how much your stay will cost, and not for the price of the room; you can, of course, ask for the rate for the room.

Here are some more examples:

The Manager,
Mayfair Hotel,
Thames Road,
Broadworth,
Goss-shire,
England JE5 0AJ   20th April 19—

Dear Sir,
    I should like to book a single room with shower for the nights of Monday, Tuesday and Wednesday, 5th, 6th, and 7th May 19—.
    I hope to arrive at about 7 o'clock in the evening and would like to have dinner.
    Would you please let me know your current prices.

Yours faithfully,

12th April 19——

Mr T. Foggarty,
Manager,
Oatlands Hotel,
High Street,
Grantend,
England GR14 9OK

Dear Mr Foggarty,
My wife and I would very much like to stay at the Oatlands Hotel again this year, and hope you can reserve us a double room with private bath for the week beginning Saturday, 18th May, for seven nights.
We shall be leaving Greece at the end of the month, so I would be glad if you would write to me as soon as possible.
Please give our kind regards to Mrs Foggarty, and tell her we look forward to seeing her again.

Yours sincerely,

The Manager,
Mayfair Hotel,
Thames Road,
Broadworth,
Goss-shire,
England JE5 0AJ   1st May 19——

Dear Sir,
Thank you for your letter of 27th April.
Unfortunately, my plans have been changed and I should be glad if you could alter my booking for a week later, that is, Monday, Tuesday and Wednesday, 12th, 13th and 14th May 19——.
I apologize for this alteration and hope you still have vacancies for the later dates.

Yours faithfully,

Making Telephone Calls

The quickest way to get information is to telephone. Most calls can be dialled directly. You can find the correct code number from the *code book* which is given to all people who have telephones, or from the lists in public call boxes. You dial the code number followed by the number of the person or firm to whom you wish to speak. If the exchange you want is not in the code book, you must ring the *operator*, usually by dialling 100. The operator will ring the number for you.

In England it is cheaper to telephone after 6 p.m. (1800 hours) or on Saturday and Sunday. (Of course, if you are making a business call these times would not be convenient.) If you have to speak to one person in particular, it may be better to make a Personal Call. You make this call by dialling 100 for the operator, giving her the name of the person to whom you wish to speak. The call will then not be charged until you are actually speaking to that person, although a charge is made for the service. You can do this if you are trying to find someone in a large office, or someone who may be out when you telephone.

When the telephonist at the firm you are ringing answers, she will probably say 'Jones and Company, good morning', You then ask for the person to whom you wish to speak: 'May I speak to Mr Johnson, please' or 'May I speak to the Sales Manager, please'. His secretary will probably answer and will ask who you are before she puts you through. The conversation might go like this:

'Mr Johnson's office.'

'May I speak to Mr Johnson, please?'

'Who is calling, please?'

'It is Mr Jensen from Sweden.'

'Just one moment please, and I'll connect you.'

And you will then speak to Mr Johnson.

You may be asked to spell a name or word, and to save time and trouble it is advisable to use the normal way of spelling as listed below. (Although there are variations which are perfectly acceptable, you must make sure that they cannot be confused with any other letter.)

A for Apple
B for Butter, Bernard, Birmingham or Benjamin
C for Charlie
D for David
E for Edward
F for Frederick
G for George
H for Harry (remember 'H' is an aspirate in
    English, not silent as in the French for 'hotel', and
    in some countries it is pronounced 'haich'.)
I for Isaac
J for John or Jack
K for King
L for London
M for Mother or Mary
N for Nothing, Nuts or Nellie
O for Orange
P for Peter
Q for Queen
R for Robert
S for Samuel
T for Tommy
U for Uncle
V for Victor
W for William
X for X-ray
Y for Yellow
Z for Zebra

When you give numbers, 0 can be spoken as either *nought* or
zero. Make sure you distinguish very carefully between 5 (five)
and 9 (nine).

Sending Telegrams and Telexes

To send an inland telegram today you have to dictate it over the
telephone. (You will find the number to ring at the beginning of
the code book). To send an overseas telegram you can also write
out your message on a special form you can get at any post office.

But today most companies use telexes. To send a telex you find the code of the recipient in a telex directory, type the message onto a special punch tape, which you then insert into the machine after dialling the code you need, and wait for the answer if necessary.

With both of these methods each word costs money, so you will make your message as short as possible. Do not, however, make it so short as to be confusing – for instance 'CANNOT COME MON WILL TUES' Does this mean '. . . will come Tuesday' or '. . . will Tuesday be convenient'?

```
MAYHOTEL 823721 GS
DARCHOC 627754 G LIVERPOOL 3.6.82 0955
ATTN MANAGER

CANCEL ROOM 9 TO 13 JUNE.
PLEASE BOOK 16 TO 20 JUNE.

JENSEN
DARLINGS CHOCOLATE COMPANY
LIVERPOOL
823721 GS
627754 G
```

Doing it this way the text is about 3 lines longer than at present but the telex is more compact than the present telegram form.

Making Appointments

It is always sensible to arrange to see the person with whom you wish to discuss business. You should write to him to make an appointment. You can, of course, do this from your own country, but you may not know the details of your trip until you are in England. Do not forget that you do not need to put 'England' on your correspondent's address (either in the letter or on the envelope) if you are in the country! You will be able to get headed notepaper* from your hotel:

Mr A. Johnson,
Sales Manager,
Quadco Factory Ltd.,
Coventry Road,
Market Highing,
West Midlands EG7 2TH   5th May 19—

Dear Mr Johnson,
   I represent the Seinhof Fabriken Gesellschaft, makers of
machine tools, and I would like to talk to you about
purchasing some of the components* you make.
   I shall be in Birmingham for a week and would like to see
you. Would Wednesday, 12th May, at 1100 hours be
convenient?
   I shall be at this hotel all week and a message or letter
will reach me here.

Yours sincerely,

L. Fischer

L. Fischer
Overseas Representative

Or you may not know who you need to see, so you can write to
the Sales Manager:

The Sales Manager,
Jones and Son,
193 East High Street,
London E17 9ST   11th October 19 —

Dear Sir,
   I come from the Soyan Electronic Company in Tokyo,
and will be in London from next Tuesday to Friday,
(18th–21st October). I should like to call on you to discuss
our new transistorized colour television sets. Would 0930
hours on Wednesday, 19th October be convenient?
   I shall be in Birmingham, at the Albion Hotel, from
Wednesday, 12th October, until next Monday (17th), and a
message there will reach me. If the day or the time is not
convenient, will you please suggest another.
   I look forward to hearing from you,

Yours faithfully,

T. Isuzo

T. Isuzo
Managing Director

The reply will simply be a note or a phone call, saying that the time is convenient or suggesting another time:

Dear Mr Isuzo,
   Thank you for your letter.
   I shall be very pleased to see you and discuss your new transistorized colour television sets. I am afraid I cannot manage 9.30 a.m.* on Wednesday, but I could manage 9.30 a.m. on Thursday, 20th October. I hope this will be convenient for you.
   I look forward to meeting you.

Yours sincerely,

PWest

P. West
Sales Manager

Here are some more examples:

The Manager,
Thornley Bookshops Ltd.,
15 Bannold Street,
Hodgeston,
Essex RD4 2LK   30th May 19—

Dear Sir,
   I am at present in England visiting bookshops with a view to making known our new type of map for use in Europe.
   I shall be in Hodgeston on Wednesday, 20th June, and should like to call on you at 2.30 p.m.* on that day.
   If I do not hear from you to the contrary, I shall assume that it will be convenient for me to call at that time.

Yours faithfully,

If you have called at this bookshop many times before you may know the Manager quite well (perhaps you have become quite good friends), in which case you might write a more personal letter starting:

14th June 19—

Dear John,
    I shall be in Hodgeston again on Wednesday, 20th June, and would like to call to see you at Bannold Street. We have just printed some new maps which might interest you.
    I hope to be with you at about 2.30 p.m. I have several other calls to make so shall probably not finish work until about 5.30 p.m. I should be delighted if you and your wife would join me for a drink at The Mitre at 6.30 p.m.
    I look forward to seeing you again.

Yours,

Note: In a letter to a friend, the usual ending is 'Yours,' leaving out 'sincerely'. But you must know your friend well enough to use his first name if you end the letter this way.

Exercises

1 Say the following telephone numbers out loud:
(a) 01 229 9982
(b) 06 130 76021
(c) 76 55932
(d) 94 12975
(e) 024 036 9418

2 (a) Write to the Portman Hotel, Bull Square, Manchester MA56 7LA, and book a room for yourself for four nights beginning on 9th October.
  (b) You are Mr J. Duncan, the Manager of the hotel. Reply to the last letter, making the reservation.*

(c) While you are staying at this hotel, write to the Exeter Hotel, 99 Old Heath Lane, Birmingham BM17 0QC, to book a room from 13th October for a week.

(d) Write the letter that Mr John Smith, the Manager of the Exeter Hotel, writes to confirm the reservation.

3 (a) Write to Mr R. Morton, the Sales Manager of McDonald and Co., 55 Canning Street, Manchester MN5 3VC, asking if you can come and see him to discuss selling some goods made by your firm, while you are in Manchester. (See Exercise 2a.)

(b) You are the Sales Manager of McDonald and Co. Write to confirm the appointment.

(c) You are staying at the Exeter Hotel in Birmingham. The Small Oak Metal Works Ltd., at 183 High Street, Small Heath, Birmingham BM25 8PM, makes machine tools and you hope to import some into your own country, for use in your business. Write and make an appointment to talk about this.

(d) You are Mr T. Moult, the Sales Manager of the Small Oak Metal Works Ltd. Write and suggest a time two days later than the date mentioned, as you will be away on that day.

(e) Answer Mr Moult's letter.

4 Put the following information in a short form, suitable for a telegram:

(a) You have booked a room in a hotel for four nights, beginning Tuesday, 12th February. You would like to come on Monday instead and stay five nights.

(b) Change an appointment you have made for Friday, 5th March, at 10.30 to Thursday, 4th March, at 15.30.

(c) Unexpectedly you will be able to visit the Sales Manager of Smith Chemical Works on 4th January at any time convenient to him.

(d) Reply to (c), suggesting 3.30 p.m. (You should change this to the 24-hour clock when you reply.)

(e) You are unable to go to Manchester and must therefore cancel your appointment for 10.30 tomorrow morning.

5 Role-playing in class:

You are telephoning the Sales Manager of Jones' Metal Factory.

(a) Hold the conversation you will have with the telephonist of the firm. (Another student or your teacher should take the part of the telephonist.)

(b) The telephonist connects you with the Sales Manager's secretary. Explain who you are to her, and ask to be put through to him.

Glossary

@: sign for 'at'.

a.m. (from Latin *ante meridiem*): the time before noon (i.e. 0000 to 1200 hrs).

account:
> *to open an account:* to arrange credit.
> *to settle an account:* to pay money owed under a credit arrangement.

agency: the business of an agent.
> *a sole agency/agent:* the only organization/person acting for someone else in one kind of business, or in one area.

available: can be obtained.

balance (of an account): the amount remaining to be paid.
> *balance carried forward:* balance already in existence.

body (of a letter): the main part of the letter.

branch (of a firm): one of the firm's offices or factories.

to do business (with someone): to buy from or sell to someone.
> *terms of business:* arrangements for payment, discount, delivery involved in a business transaction.
> *favourable terms:* these are good for the customer.

commission: money paid to an agent, usually a percentage of the money received for the goods he sells. The goods belong to the agent.

commodity: something used in trade.

component: a part of something.

consignment: something sent from one person to another.
> *on consignment:* something sent to an agent to be sold for as high a price as possible. The agent pays only for what he sells, and only after he has sold it. The rest of the goods belong to the supplier.

under separate cover: sent separately, usually separately from a letter or an invoice.

credit: if somebody gets goods and need not pay for them till later, the goods are said to be *on credit*. This system is one of credit terms.
> *in credit:* there is more money in the account than is needed to pay bills.
> *to give (a) credit:* to allow money wrongly paid to be used to pay a later bill.
> *credit-worthy:* safe for a certain amount of money.

current (adj.): up-to-date, correct now.

to deal in (something): to keep a supply of, sell.

delivery date: the date when something leaves the seller (sometimes when it actually reaches the customer, but it is not often used this way in foreign trade).

despatched: sent (the packing has been done, the documents obtained, and the article has left the sender).

directors (of a firm): the group who manage the business of a company.

discount: if a firm pays cash for something, or pays within a certain time, it can usually pay less than the full price. The reduction is called *the trade discount*, or *discount*.

documents: papers used as a written record of something. They are usually printed.

fee: sum of money, usually decided earlier, paid to someone for doing something.

printed form: a printed piece of paper which can be quickly filled in and used instead of a letter – for instance, when ordering something (when an *order form* is used).

freight: goods being moved somewhere; the cost of doing this.

goods: things (to be bought, sold, sent, etc.).

leaflet: a printed piece of paper giving information about something, a brochure.

market: number of people who may buy something, often in a given place.

marketing: the theory and practice of selling.

M/V: Merchant Vessel (used when goods are sent by sea).

Middle East: includes Iran, Turkey, Lebanon, Jordan, Syria, Egypt, Saudi Arabia.

No.: Number.

notepaper:

    printed notepaper: paper for writing letters with the address, telephone number, and other information such as the name of the manager, the name and type of the business, and the telex number printed at the top of it.

    headed notepaper: another term for printed notepaper.

to operate as: to be.

ordinal numbers: showing position in a series – 1st, 2nd, etc.

p.m. (from Latin *post meridiem*): afternoon (from 1200 to 2359 hrs.).

per: for each (per day = each day).

private and confidential: usually used when making enquiries about some-one's personal qualities, such as honesty, or his credit-worthiness. It means that no one will be told that the enquiry is being made, and that the answer will not be told to anyone else.

product: something which is made or manufactured by man or machines.

Purchase Order: an official order to buy something (usually on a printed form).

quality: how good (or bad) something is.

quantity: number, amount.

quarterly: every 3 months (a quarter of a year).

range: distance between one limit and another; class of goods.

    a wide range: one in which there is a lot of difference between the smallest and largest, or the cheapest and most expensive.

reasonable (price): not expensive for its quality.

trade and bank references: a letter from a firm or a bank explaining that you are credit-worthy for at least a certain sum.

    Your Ref. MZ/VF/7540: figures and letters like these are often found at the beginning of a letter, and refer to the sender's filing system. They usually indicate who wrote the letter, when, and about what. It is always wise to use the reference in your reply, and you may wish to add your own.

refund: the return of a sum of money (used as a noun or verb).

to represent: to be an agent for someone, to act for someone.

72

(hotel) reservation: to arrange to have a room kept for one.

retailer: someone who sells goods in small quantities to the general public, usually a shopkeeper.

stamped addressed envelope (s.a.e.): In England, the sender of a letter will often enclose a stamped envelope addressed to himself, which can be used for the reply. Compare *International Reply Coupon*, which does the same thing from one country to another. (This is a form which can be bought in one country and sent to another to be exchanged for stamps.)

to stock: to keep a supply of something.

   stocks: supplies.

terms: see *business.*

in transit: on a journey.

to transact business: to carry out business.

warehouse: large building used by firms for storing large (bulk) supplies of their products. It may be a long way from the place where the products are made. Agents representing a firm in a foreign country will often try to obtain warehouse space so that they can supply customers quickly.

wholesaler: one who sells goods, usually in large quantities, to somebody who will sell them again to the general public, as a retailer.

   wholesale price: this price is lower than the price the public must pay for small quantities.

would like: polite form of *want.* It should always be used instead of want, which almost always seems rude, unless it is used emphatically.